A Note to Parents

DK READERS is a compelling program for beginning readers, designed in conjunction with leading literacy experts, including Dr. Linda Gambrell, Distinguished Professor of Education at Clemson University. Dr. Gambrell has served as President of the National Reading Conference, the College Reading Association, and the International Reading Association.

Beautiful illustrations and superb full-color photographs combine with engaging, easy-to-read stories to offer a fresh approach to each subject in the series. Each DK READER is guaranteed to capture a child's interest while developing his or her reading skills, general knowledge, and love of reading.

The five levels of DK READERS are aimed at different reading abilities, enabling you to choose the books that are exactly right for your child:

Pre-level 1: Learning to read
Level 1: Beginning to read
Level 2: Beginning to read alone
Level 3: Reading alone
Level 4: Proficient readers

The "normal" age at which a child begins to read can be anywhere from three to eight years old. Adult participation through the lower levels is very helpful for providing encouragement, discussing storylines, and sounding out unfamiliar words.

No matter which level you select, you can be sure that you are helping your child learn to read, then read to learn!

LONDON, NEW YORK, MUNICH,
MELBOURNE, and DELHI

Editorial Assistant Ruth Amos
Design Assistant Satvir Sihota
Jacket Designer Liam Drane
Senior Editor Victoria Taylor
Pre-Production Producer Siu Yin Chan
Producer Louise Daly
Reading Consultant Dr. Linda Gambrell
Design Manager Nathan Martin
Publishing Manager Julie Ferris
Art Director Ron Stobbart
Publishing Director Simon Beecroft

First published in the United States in 2013
by DK Publishing
375 Hudson Street
New York, New York 10014
10 9 8 7 6 5 4 3 2 1

DK books are available at special discounts when
purchased in bulk for sales promotions, premiums,
fund-raising, or educational use.
For details, contact:
DK Publishing Special Markets
375 Hudson Street
New York, New York 10014
SpecialSales@dk.com

A catalog record for this book is available
from the Library of Congress.

ISBN: 978-1-4654-0863-1 (Paperback)
ISBN: 978-1-4654-0864-8 (Hardcover)

Printed and bound by L.Rex, China
Color reproduction in the UK by Altaimage

Discover more at

www.dk.com

Contents

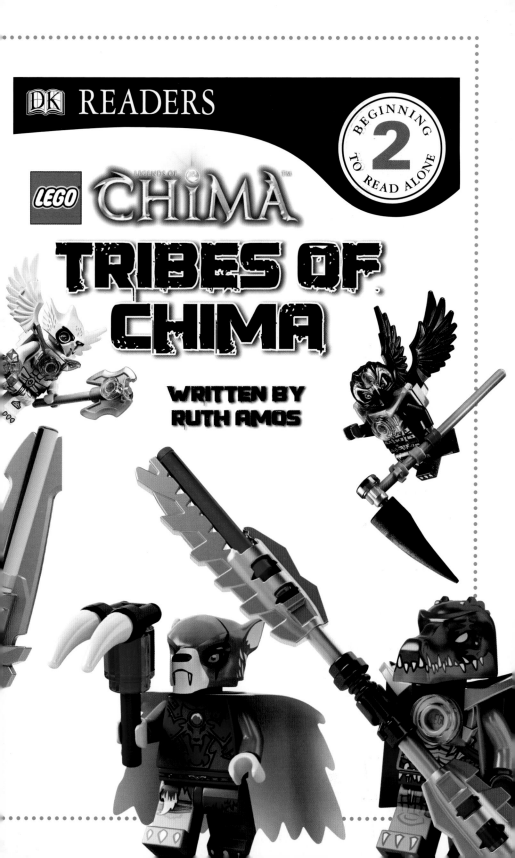

DK READERS

BEGINNING TO READ ALONE
2

LEGO LEGENDS OF CHIMA™

TRIBES OF CHIMA

WRITTEN BY RUTH AMOS

Welcome to Chima!

This is the land of Chima. Chima is a beautiful kingdom with jungles, mountains, and rivers. Many animals live here.

Chima used to be peaceful, but now big battles have erupted. The animals are fighting over a magical energy source called CHI.

CHI

CHI is found in the Sacred Pool. All the animals want to collect CHI because it is very powerful.

The animal tribes

The animals' ancestors walked on four legs like normal animals. Some of the ancestors drank CHI and started to walk on two legs.

They formed tribes and created amazing buildings and vehicles.

Crocodile   Wolf   Lion

Eagle

Raven

Today, some
of the tribes in
Chima are the
Crocodiles, Wolves,
Lions, Eagles, and Ravens.

The tribes were once friends,
but now trouble is brewing.
Who should get the most CHI?

The Lion Tribe

   Let's meet some of the tribes!
The Lion Tribe is the noblest
tribe of all.

The Lions are the sworn
guardians of the CHI.
They distribute it to
the other animals
every month.

Longtooth

Lennox

The Lions are always very
fair and they follow Chima's
laws. They all live in the
splendid Lion City.

Laval

**Longtooth
drives the
Royal Fighter
vehicle.**

Leonidas

Longtooth and Laval

Longtooth is an old foot soldier in the Lion Tribe. He has fought in many battles, but now he prefers talking to fighting. Longtooth tells Prince Laval long stories about his battles.

Longtooth

Laval only pretends to listen!
Flame-haired Laval is brave,
but he is headstrong.
One day Laval will be King
of the Lions,
but for now
he is just a
big kid at
heart!

Laval

The Crocodile Tribe

The Crocodiles are sneaky, slippery scoundrels.

They are scary-looking, with tough, scaly skin and sharp teeth.

King Crominus

Crooler

Cragger's Command Ship is green and mean!

The Crocodiles were once friends with the Lions, but now they are enemies. The Crocodiles live in swamps.

Cragger

Crominus and Cragger

King Crominus is the Crocodile leader, and he is Cragger's father. Crominus is a tough ruler, who uses logic to protect his tribe. He wears a golden helmet and a chest plate.

Royal helmet

14 59454

03 ©LEGO

Curved
red blade

King Crominus

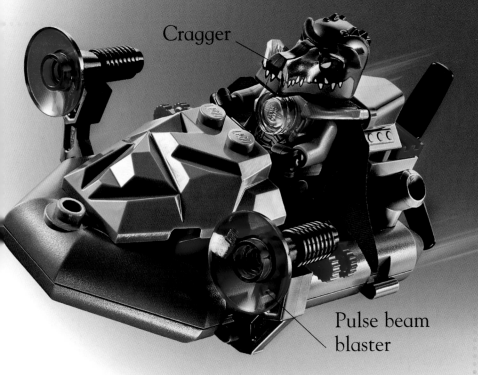

Cragger

Pulse beam blaster

Cragger is the young Prince of the Crocodile Tribe. Cragger is very greedy and is desperate to get his claws on more CHI.

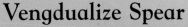

Vengdualize Spear

Cragger's favorite weapon is his golden Vengdualize spear. The blades can spin like a chain saw.

Eris pilots the Eagle Interceptor.

Eglor

Eris

Ewar

Equila

The Eagle Tribe

The Eagles are intelligent
and thoughtful creatures.
They are always talking
and discussing ideas.
Sometimes the other animals
call the Eagles "airheads"
because they can seem quite
dreamy and vague.
They just really love thinking!

The Eagles are loyal allies
of the Lion Tribe.
They live high up in the sky on
the rocky cliffs.

Eris and Eglor

Clever and kind,
Eris the Eagle loves
solving puzzles.

She is great at inventing
new battle tactics, but Eris
would prefer all the tribes to
be friends!

Eglor is the Eagles' famous
"gadget bird."
This brainy
inventor
knows all
about vehicles and armor.

Eglor loves riding
his chariot, which is
called a Speedor.
Here he is trying to
land his Speedor on
a treetop nest target.

The Raven Tribe

The Ravens are sly and deceitful birds. They love to steal things. They even steal from their friends, as well as their enemies!

Rizzo

Razcal flies the Glider.

The Ravens are allies of
the Crocodile Tribe.
They live in messy Nest Forts
that are like mazes inside.
It's best not to visit—you may
never find your way out!

Razcal

Razar

Rizzo and Rawzom

Rizzo is the scruffiest Raven.
He has tattered feathers,
a silver eye patch, and a peg leg.
But Rizzo doesn't care.
He's got things to steal!
He pinches things with his
Grabberatus claw tool.

Grabbing claw

Rizzo

Rawzom

Scary beak-shaped
scythe

Rawzom
is the King of
the Ravens.
Rawzom is strong, but
silent—he doesn't say much.
When he does grunt, the other
Ravens know it's best to obey him!

The Wolf Tribe

The Wolves are ferocious, but they are also practical. The Wolves will always think of the pack first, before themselves. The Wolf Tribe is an ally of the Crocodile Tribe.

The Wolves live and work in battle vehicles, and roam around Chima in a pack. They all cram into the vehicles together, so life is rather cramped and very smelly!

Winzar

akz

Wakz's
Pack Tracker
is a scary sight.

Winzar and Wilhurt

Winzar is only a young Wolf, but he is full of energy. He is always starting silly scraps with other animals.

Winzar wields his own CHI-powered black ax.

Battle wounds
Winzar lost an eye and gained his nasty red scars during one of his many fights!

Wilhurt is a mean and
dangerous brute!
His two favorite things are
fighting and hunting.
He spends all day stalking prey
with his big black ax.

Powerful blue
Speedor Wheel

Watch out, Wilhurt!

The good guys

The Lion Tribe and the Eagle Tribe are allies who protect each other in Chima's battles.

The Lions and the Eagles have invented many weapons. Ewar has a pulse beam cannon. Laval wields a golden sword. It is nearly as big as he is!

Laval

Ewar

Pulse beam cannon

Double-bladed ax is swift and sharp.

Eglor

Eris

The bad guys

The naughty Crocodiles, Ravens, and Wolves want to seize more power. They are greedy for more CHI. These bad guys have formed a team to attack the Lions and Eagles.

Metal eye patch

Quiz

1. Which tribe does Eglor belong to?

2. Who are the sworn guardians of the CHI?

3. Which tribe likes to steal things?

4. What is the name of Cragger's favorite weapon?

5. What is this vehicle called?

1. Eagle Tribe, 2. Lion Tribe, 3. Raven Tribe, 4. Vengdualize, 5. Wakz's Pack Tracker

Who knows what will become
of the kingdom of Chima?
Which tribes will be victorious?
Only time can tell…

A red CHI
crystal glows on
King Crominus's
royal ax.